His Glory Is Greater

D1355541

DEBBIE GALBRAITH

NEWMAN SPRINGS PUBLISHING
320 Broad Street
Red Bank, NJ 07701

First originally published by Newman
Springs Publishing 2020

ISBN 978-1-64801-972-2 (Paperback)
ISBN 978-1-64801-973-9 (Digital)

Printed in the United States of America

CONTENTS

INTRODUCTION

His Glory is greater! As I was reading the Bible and spending time with God in the quiet of my home, these words came up in my spirit. Along with them was the understanding that it would be the title of a book. Rather than accepting the title as is, I began rehearsing circumstances both great and small (His glory is greater than this situation or circumstance; His glory is greater than that situation or circumstance, and so on, trying to make it complete). Then I said to God, in anything and everything, You are greater. You are the Maker of heaven and earth and all that is within. You are the potter; we are the clay. The created thing cannot be greater than the Creator. Your glory is greater. Then the words *I am* came to my remembrance. With that, I understood and I knew I had the complete title. I responded by saying, "Yes, You Are! You are the great I Am; the same yesterday, today, and forever. *His Glory Is Greater*! A complete sentence—the complete title. Just as He referred to Himself as *I am*, I understood His glory is greater. The same! An all-encompassing statement of knowledge and truth.

I began reflecting more on what God says about Himself—who He is and the traits of His character and spirit. He said in Exodus 34, "I proclaim Myself to be gracious and merciful, longsuffering, abounding in goodness and truth." To abound in anything does not allow room for the contrary. If it is in opposition, it has no part. If full, there is no room for more. That substance can overflow, but no opposing substance can be found.

Nehemiah said, "He Is Great, Mighty, and Awesome." Full of wonder!

In James we learn that "wisdom from above is first of all pure, then peaceable, gentle, willing to yield, full of mercy and good fruits, without partiality and without hypocrisy." Also, "wisdom which is not from above is self-seeking and brings about confusion and every evil work." An evil work is not from above—not from God. There is no room in God's wisdom, being, or character for evil.

Galatians 5:22–23 tells us that "the fruit of His Spirit is love, joy, peace, longsuffering, kindness, goodness, faithfulness, gentleness, self-control."

Then in Malachi 3:16, "I Am the Lord, I do not change."

WORRY NOT

It had just begun to rain that August day. The sun was still shining through the clouds. The rain shower was refreshing and relaxing, adding to the expectation of vacation scheduled to begin the following day. The moisture had apparently caused the pavement to become slick. As I drove through the intersection, the traffic light turned yellow; and, glancing to my right, I noticed a policeman at the scene of an accident. Then looking into the rearview mirror, I saw a car coming through the intersection a short distance behind me. The light was now obviously red.

My thought immediately went to the policeman at the intersection, then just as quickly, I dismissed it from my thinking. Looking forward, I continued toward home which was only one mile ahead. Suddenly, my car was struck on the passenger side. Apparently, the driver of the vehicle which had come through the intersection behind me attempted to come around my vehicle and lost control of his vehicle on the slick pavement. My body and head were thrown uncontrollably side to side against the driver side window and door, and backward and forward between the steering wheel and seat. When I stopped and looked into the rearview mirror, the other vehicle was still swerving, circling out of control and thrown backward by the force of motion onto the curb and into the center median.

Once the other vehicle came to a stop, I got out of my car and began to walk toward it. I noticed my entire body shaking as though there was an inner tremor from head to toe. Quickly assessing the situation, I realized I was not experiencing anxiety or fear, and there was no apparent injury. Then, I recalled stories of adrenaline rushes in certain situations and thought that must be what I was experiencing.

The other driver got out of his car and approached me. I immediately recalled the policeman working the accident and I thought perhaps the officer witnessed the impact and would respond to the situation. I suggested we walk across the street and telephone the police. Rather than responding to my suggestion, he asked for my insurance information. After assuring him the information was in my car, I once again stated that we needed to telephone the police and file a report. He turned and began to walk back toward his car saying, "Let me get—" Never completing his sentence, he got into his car and drove away. As he pulled out and drove around me, I attempted to get the tag number from the vehicle only to notice there was not a license plate on the car. Later, the police speculated it to be a stolen vehicle.

Though very physically shaken, the tests and X-rays at the trauma center did not indicate a concussion, serious injury, or broken bones. I was diagnosed with bruises and strained muscles. Being released with the recommended treatment of rest and muscle relaxants for the apparent spasms, we continued with vacation plans. A rental vehicle was acquired and we proceeded, expecting a full recovery. However, as the vacation progressed, so did the pain and the swelling in my body. Thinking perhaps the muscle relaxant which had been prescribed was the cause, we located a clinic and explained our situation. The doctor wrote a prescription for a different type of muscle relaxant, but he could not explain the symptoms.

I could not walk, especially in the sand, without my muscles aching. After only a few steps, it was as though I had lifted weights to the point of fatigue, and each step after was like that one more rep requiring total focus and determination, usually with the assistance of another. With that, we phoned a pain specialist in our hometown to have an appointment in place when we returned.

Even then, our focus was not on my physical condition but on our time together. I maintained an attitude of gratitude for that time together which showed forth in joy, peace, and childlike fun; a time which will always be remembered as good and never suffering.

I reflected on the time as a sixth-grader when the desire to visit Cape Cod was so firmly planted in me after some reading. It was in the car on the highway as we were driving to Cape Cod that the Lord came so closely with his loving presence to let me know He was fulfilling that desire. And the words *worry not* were so instilled in me that I had to acknowledge God, let Him know I had heard, and then act on it.

When my body began to swell and my clothes no longer fit properly, I worried not. When I could not walk from one point to another without several rest stops, I worried not. When we had unexpected expenses, I worried not. Then, when the hurricane was forecasted, the Cape Cod businesses, houses, and cottages were being boarded up, vehicles were lined up bumper to bumper for miles on the highway exiting the area, and my husband wanted to stay to help the owner of the cottages board up the property where we were residing, I worried not. Numerous incidents occurred which Satan attempted to use to steal that special time, but acting in faith on the word of God, allowed it to be a treasured experience. From the cottage on the beach to the shops, lighthouse, day trip to Nantucket, and ferry by Martha's Vineyard, even the simplest pleasures, such as coffee and lunches in the cottage, were magnified. I knew what Satan meant for harm, God would turn to the good of those who love Him and are called according to His purpose. And He will never leave me nor forsake me. Also, I could reflect on that time in the car with God, acknowledge the words, worry not, and continue in faith and obedience.

Jesus tells us in Matthew 6:33–34 to "seek first the Kingdom of God [on earth as it is in heaven] and His Righteousness [we are made righteous through

Jesus Christ], and all these things shall be added to you. Therefore, do not worry about tomorrow, for tomorrow will worry about its own things. Sufficient for the day is its own trouble."

Jesus told us to live one day at a time—literally, now is enough. God is always faithful. I find that when I think on my time of salvation, I can go to a place of gratitude and thanksgiving which leads me to the knowledge that He cares for me. Jesus said, "Nevertheless do not rejoice in this, that the spirits are subject to you, but rejoice that your names are recorded in heaven" (Luke 10:20 NKJ).

I cannot give thought to those things that cause worry or fear; I must look beyond to the answer and focus my thoughts on those things. I must stay fixed on what is true. Worry time is wasted time and energy. He tells us that not one of us by worry can add one cubit to our stature.

God feeds the birds of the air and we are much more valuable than they. He clothes the lilies of the field which grow and neither toil nor spin. That even Solomon in all his glory was not arrayed like one of them. God cared enough to clothe the grass of the field which is here today and thrown into the oven tomorrow. Its purpose is short-lived and for our benefit. Then Jesus asks, Will God not much more clothe you?

When I meditate in these things, I know He has a plan, and He will take care of me and show me my part. He will give me steps to take and lead me each step of the way. I will be strong in the Lord and in the power of His might and stay away from wrong thoughts.

> Be anxious for nothing, but in everything by prayer and sup-plication, with thanksgiving, let your requests be made known to God; and the peace of God, which surpasses all understand-ing, will guard your hearts and minds through Christ Jesus. Finally, brethren, whatever things are true, whatever things are noble, whatever things are just, whatsoever things are pure, what-soever things are lovely, whatso-ever things are of good report, if there is any virtue and if there is anything praiseworthy—medi-

tate on these things. (Philippians 4:6–8 NKJ)

Philippians 4:13 reads, "I can do all things through Christ who strengthens me."

Pillars Built on a Firm Foundation

The first morning home after vacation, I awoke to the sound of my four-year-old granddaughter talking and playing in the living room and my husband and daughter visiting. This was a new experience for me. I had routinely been the first one up over the years and would never have considered staying in bed knowing someone was visiting in my home; however, this morning was different.

My first desire was to join them in the living room. After all, I hadn't seen either of them in several weeks. Especially after hearing my granddaughter ask if she could go to my bedroom, I wanted nothing more than to call for her to come into my room. Resisting the temptation, I soon encountered intense spiritual warfare.

The pain was so severe it seemed to pierce the very center of my bones. Then I found myself battling thoughts of bone cancer. Scripture would come to my remembrance and I prayed, thanking God that I knew Him and knew that "I was redeemed from the curse of the law. Jesus took my infirmities and bore my sicknesses and diseases." Knowing that I "wrestled not against flesh and blood but against powers and principalities in heavenly places" and for knowing that "we are to seek the Lord first and all these things shall be added." I began meditating on Jesus, quietly speaking thanksgiving for specific things he had made possible in my life.

I thanked Him for my salvation, for calling me out of darkness and into His light, for those who had prayed for me and then acted by reaching out to me and my family. I was fifteen years old, a sophomore in high school. As I lay in my bed in the quiet of the night, the Holy Spirit entered my room. His presence was so real; but, at the time, I didn't know anything about the Holy Spirit or conviction. I had heard about Jesus in Sunday school classes over the years but never learned about accepting Him as Savior. We moved a lot so there was no consistency in attending Sunday school or developing lasting relationships, and I had only attended a few church services in my life.

When the Holy Spirit entered, I felt such remorse, and I cried, "God, I'm sorry! I'm sorry! I'm sorry!" I did not know why I was sorry. I just felt so undone and lost; I knew I wasn't right in His presence. It still amazes me how I felt no real fear of such an awesome presence, only a piercing awareness of truth.

The next night, I experienced the same presence, and again, desperately said, "God, I'm sorry; I'm sorry." The third night, I asked God to show me what I could do. I was so terribly uncomfortable laying in the still of the night, knowing I was undone in God's sight, and not knowing what to do about it. The following day, which was a Friday, as I was stepping off the school bus (I truly believe the first and only time I was the last person off the bus), the driver stopped me and asked if I was a Christian. I didn't really understand what he was asking me, so I responded *no*. He then asked about my mom, dad, brothers, and sisters. He said there was a revival at his church (he was a pastor of a local church) and asked me to tell my parents he would drive out on Saturday for a visit. We lived twelve miles west of town on an extremely curvy road which bordered a lake; so a person truly had to go out of his way to get there.

When he visited on Saturday, my mom committed to attend church on Sunday with us kids. That visit resulted in four lives receiving Jesus as Savior (my mom, my older brother and my younger brother, as well as myself). Afterward, as I rode home in the car, I noticed there was such a filling, not feeling, of peace and contentment in me. I recalled being so hungry during the church service. Now, as snacks were being passed around in the car, I realized the fullness I had within. I was so satisfied; I just wanted to dwell on my newfound peace.

I will forever be grateful for those who prayed for me, for those who took time to reach out to me and my family and show me how to relieve the burden I experienced. As I grew in the Lord, I also experienced seeing other members of my family transformed and grow in the Lord. It was a brand-new life!

That is the time I could reflect on to know I was redeemed from the curse of the law. That was the firm foundation of Jesus Christ!

I remembered the woman caught in adultery. The law said she would be stoned; Jesus redeemed her from the curse of the law when He said, "Let the one among you who is without sin cast the first stone." Not one stepped forward; then Jesus said, "Neither do I condemn you. Go and sin no more" (John 8:1–11). In addition, I had learned from the Word that Jesus took my infirmities and bore my sicknesses and diseases. He had been "wounded for my transgressions, bruised for my iniquities, chastised for my peace, and by His stripes I was healed."

One by one, I recalled God's work in my life. His grace, mercy, and faithfulness established pillars of faith on the firm foundation of Jesus Christ. I found strength in reflecting on these times during this time of great physical need. Just as David encouraged himself in the Lord, I used these times to build myself up and be strong in the Lord.

> Now David was greatly distressed, for the people spoke of stoning him, because the soul of all the people was grieved [bitter in spirit], every man for his sons and daughters. But David strengthened [encouraged] himself in the Lord his God. (1 Samuel 30:6)

I remember a few days after accepting Jesus as my Savior and Lord when the preacher asked my mom if she had noticed any changes in me. Her immediate response was that I wasn't getting angry like I had been doing previously. I didn't even realize it until she mentioned it; but the anger had disappeared. It had been overtaken by the love, peace, and contentment God brought into my life.

Jesus is the Bread of Life, Living Water. Years later I saw the significance of Jesus being born in a manger—a trough used for feeding and watering animals. I knew God could have made the best room in the inn available to Mary and Joseph if that had been His plan. Instead, Jesus was laid in a manger. The definition of the word trough is a channel or conduit for conveying food or water. Jesus was the substance placed in that trough as our Bread of Life; Living Water. In John 6:35, Jesus said "I Am the Bread of Life. He who comes to Me shall never hunger, and he who believes in Me shall never thirst." Continuing in verse 40, He says, "This is the will of Him who sent Me, that everyone who sees the Son and believes in Him may have everlasting life; and I will raise Him up at the last day."

Again, in John 6:48, "I Am the Bread of Life." Then He continues in verse 49 & 51: "Your fathers ate the manna in the wilderness, and are dead. I Am the Living Bread which came down from Heaven. If anyone eats of this Bread, he will live forever; and the Bread that I shall give is My Flesh, which I shall give for the life of the world."

In John 7:37–38, Jesus said, "If anyone thirsts, let him come to Me and drink. He who believes in Me, as the Scripture has said, out of his heart [spirit; belly; innermost being] will flow rivers of living water."

When Jesus was speaking with the woman at the well in John 4:13–14, He answered and said to her, "Whoever drinks of this water [the well water] will thirst again, but whoever drinks of the water that I shall give him will never thirst. But the water that I shall give him will become in him a fountain of water springing up into everlasting life."

He shall give His angels charge
over you, to keep you in all your
ways (Psalms 91:11)

As a teenager in my early driving days, I became too comfortable and familiar with my drive home and began daydreaming. As I drove from town to our home on the lake, I approached a curve, traveling too fast. I was entering the curve before I realized it, and if I didn't make the curve, I was going straight ahead over the treetops and into the lake. Suddenly, I felt the steering wheel as it turned through my hands. It was as though I was not holding it; it turned without my assistance. My hands remained still, and the steering wheel slipped through them. Not only did I make the curve, but my vehicle remained in my lane of traffic, never crossing over the double-yellow lines, never skidding; just a smooth turn around an approximately ninety-degree curve to my right. I most definitely had an angel assisting me that day! Here I am years later, still in awe of that experience!

Again I say to you that if two of
you agree on earth concerning
anything that they ask, it will be
done for them by My Father in
Heaven. For where two or three
are gathered together in My
Name, I am there in the midst of
them. (Matthew 18:19–20 NKJ)

While I was still in high school, the doctor had
done all he could do medically and had given up
on my mom's life due to dehydration and bronchial
pneumonia. I remember the relatives being called in
and my brother coming home from college. When it
was my turn to go in to see her, I began to talk to her
and was told not to cause her to use her energy. As
I stood and looked at her, I saw one little tear come
into the corner of her eye. I did not realize it then,
but that one little tear allowed me to see life. I was
hearing dehydration, but I was seeing a tear. Then
during the Wednesday evening prayer service, the
pastor announced to the congregation that my family
had been told by the doctor that my mom would not
live. He called everyone to intercede on our behalf. I
remember having such a loss for words. I could not

say anything. I pressed close to Jesus and then began a very quiet moaning. I was drawn to look up, and as I did, I saw a cloud-like substance exiting the ceiling of the church building. I believe it was an angel as described in Jacob's dream in Genesis 28:12–13 where a ladder was set up on the earth and its top reached to heaven; and there the angels of God were ascending and descending on it. The Lord stood above it and said: "I am the Lord God of Abraham your father and the God of Isaac; the land on which you lie I will give to you and your descendants." In Genesis 28:16–17 Jacob awoke from his sleep and said, "Surely the Lord is in this place and I did not know it. And he was afraid and said, How awesome is this place! This is none other than the house of God, and this is the gate of Heaven!" I see prayer as that gate to heaven. "When we pray as touching anything…according to His will… We enter into His gates with thanksgiving and into His courts with praise." God's word was being spoken in a unified prayer and His messengers were at work. The next day as our pastor was by my mom's side reading Psalm 23, her life was restored. She later said as the words, "Yea, though I walk through the valley of the shadow of death I shall fear no evil" were spoken, she felt life come back into her.

Sometime later, I heard her tell someone she did not want to leave here knowing I would be robbed of having a life of my own. In her compassion, she thought as the oldest daughter, I would feel bound to help raise my younger brothers and sisters rather than pursuing a life of my own. I reflected on that tear and wondered if that was her thought as I stood beside her bed—if that thought triggered the tear. I never thought anything along those lines. It never entered my heart that she would not live, much less think about my future.

When we believe we receive when we pray, we shall have whatsoever we ask. (Matthew 21:22 NKJ)

Therefore I tell you, whatever you ask for in prayer, believe that you have received it, and it will be yours (Mark 11:24 NIV)

I asked Him to remove a mole which had appeared in such a private area I didn't want to be examined even by a physician, and the very next morning it was gone.

A migraine headache disappeared as my husband and a friend prayed.

A spirit of suicide was defeated at the onset as I pressed into Jesus rather than giving in to the thoughts.

When our older daughter was five years old, her hearing was restored. We had taken her to an ear, nose, and throat specialist when we realized her hearing was impaired. She was not hearing anything. She could read lips when face-to-face. We did not realize our four-year-old daughter was relaying messages to her. Her kindergarten teacher reported to us that she was a daydreamer and inattentive. Because she was so well-behaved and made such good grades, she was seated in the back of the class. There she could not read lips, could not interact, and was in her own little world. She didn't tell us she wasn't hearing because to her it was normal. She looked at me one day in frustration and said, *look at me so I can hear you.* That prompted my attention. After a hearing test, the physician said they would put tubes in her ears, but we would have to wait to see if the nerve damage was permanent. That evening, our pastor asked everyone to join in prayer for her hearing to be restored. After prayer, we sat down toward the front of the church. A short time afterward, someone entered the rear entrance of the sanctuary, and our daughter turned to see what it was. She then looked at me and asked what it was. I told her someone came in the door, and I asked her if she heard the door open and close. She did. Her hearing had been fully restored even before the tubes were inserted.

A broken toe was healed, and I was wearing heels to church three days later.

Over the years, God had met needs, protected, and cared for me, gave me peace in times of trouble, and one by one, one after the other, His victories came to my remembrance. Then, with boldness and confidence from my innermost being, the words *I will live!* rose up, and as I spoke those words, my spirit leaped up from the bed as my fleshly body slowly followed inch by inch.

I shall not die, but live and declare the works of the Lord.

The battle had been won, though not so that others could see or even that I could feel, but reflecting on that moment would sustain me innumerable times until the healing was known in my flesh and be acknowledged by others. A spiritual battle at the onset of any temptation or attack is crucial. Speaking the truth of God's Word to take authority over the situation brings strength and confidence during the time of battle. Do not live with regrets—begin now! I could have looked back at the scene of the accident and said, "What if I had taken authority over the tremor, what if?" Would the attack have progressed as it did? The point is I had to begin the battle as soon as I came to the realization I was being attacked to a much larger degree than I had conceived in the beginning. It did not stop with recovery from the physical, apparent signs at the time of the accident.

Soon after the above spiritual battle, I attended the appointment with the pain specialist. His first words after the initial examination were of tests which would rule out cancer, lupus, and other such diseases. At the end of the testing, it was determined and diagnosed as fibromyalgia, caused by trauma to the central nervous system. It was explained to me that though this particular disease was incurable, it did not attack major body organs. It did, however, leave people debilitated and unable to care for themselves. Some could manage longer than others, and the longer I could push myself and remain somewhat active, the longer I could delay dependency on a wheelchair and ultimately being bedridden and assisted, ending in total care. Finding the balance of exercise and rest was the key factor. It was crucial that I exercise to reduce the fluid retention and inflammation and remain somewhat mobile, at the same time not exhausting the muscles and causing such pain that it would be impossible to function. I experienced radiating pain in every part of my body and suffered severe muscle cramps and spasms, even in the top of my hands and feet. My muscles retained toxic fluid to the point that I had to wear clothes three to four sizes larger than I normally wore. Elastic waistbands soon entered my wardrobe. It was vitally necessary to exercise the muscles in an attempt to reduce the inflammation and fluid retention. Not only was the pain intense but muscle strength was lessening, causing total fatigue in a matter of steps. I remember walking across our living room not knowing if I could make it from the chair to the sofa. My neck muscles were so weak it seemed as though I was carrying a heavy weight on my shoulders. Leaning against a pillow, sofa, wall, anything that could help support it offered such relief. My arm muscles were so weak I could not hold them up for more than a few seconds. The simplest things like drying my hair or holding a book were extremely difficult, and at times, impossible tasks. Not only was holding the book strenuous but finding a workable position for my head was also challenging.

I continued following doctor's recommendations, using specialized low-impact, strength-building equipment, allowing the equipment to do most of the work, attending warm water therapy sessions, and physical therapy. Many days, the therapist would have to do all the movements for me; my muscles just would not function. It is impossible to explain how physically, mentally, and emotionally draining and complex the situation was. I was taking various medications, as many as twenty pills each day. When I felt like quitting or giving in to the pain, I could reflect on that initial spiritual battle and allow that knowledge and revelation to add the mental fortitude and determination to continue with a single next step.

I attended a few support group sessions; however, rather than building each other up and motivating and encouraging one another on how to cope and continue with life, it was an enabling group where people were constantly crying, "I can't, I can't, I can't"—where people went to receive sympathy rather than strength. Seeing it as detrimental to my healing, I chose not to attend.

God was faithful. The Holy Spirit is the most wonderful counselor! He gave me such scripture as "As a fluttering sparrow or a darting swallow, an undeserved curse will not come to rest" (Proverbs 26:2). In my mind's eye, I could see that sparrow fluttering his wings just above the ground, touching down occasionally, never landing. Eventually lifting and flying away and never coming to rest on the ground.

That is the way any destructive force from Satan is. It can strike, it can lie, it can attempt to steal, kill, or destroy any good, pleasing, or perfect thing; but God's glory is greater! An undeserved curse will not come to rest; and, when we are born-again Christians, we "are redeemed from the curse of the law" (Galatians 3:13).

There came a point in time when it was necessary to ask my doctor about receiving a handicapped parking permit. By the time I parked and walked to the storefront, I was physically exhausted. He said anything we could do to assist in keeping me mobile as long as possible, he would be happy to do. He was amazed that I was still motivated and determined to continue, and he was so supportive, always treating me with dignity and respect.

As I was exiting a store one day, I saw my physical reflection in the glass store front. I was shocked. This was an old woman, bent over, moving so slowly, and appearing so worn and tired. Then, in God's faithfulness, the Holy Spirit, as my counselor, showed me to reflect on how I saw myself. In my mind's eye, I was still youthful, agile, walking with a quick step and full of vitality. I understood what to do. With every step, I would picture myself walking, and I would walk as closely to that image as possible. It took additional concentration, but it kept me mobile, kept me from accepting the deterioration, and added to my thanksgiving for His work in my life.

I recalled the woman with the spirit of infirmity in Luke 13:11–13 & 16:

> And behold, there was a woman who had a spirit of infirmity eighteen years, and was bent over and could in no way raise herself up. But when Jesus saw her, He called her to Him and said to her, "Woman, you are loosed from your infirmity." And He laid His hands on her, and immediately she was made straight, and glorified God. So ought not this woman, being a daughter of Abraham, whom Satan has bound—think of it—for 18 years, be loosed from this bond on the Sabbath?

Then in Luke 19:9–10, Jesus said to Zacchaeus, "Today salvation has come to this house, because he also is a son of Abraham; for the Son of Man has come to seek and to save that which was lost."

Again, I was reminded of my covenant and the knowledge that Jesus took my infirmities and bore my sicknesses and diseases.

PEACE, COMFORT, COURAGE

In the midst of this physical battle, my husband of twenty-eight years passed away. This man who I had seen win spiritual battle after spiritual battle and grow from glory to glory; who, after years, had found the true knowledge and revelation of grace, determined to overcome obstacles and challenges so his daughters would not have those same battles. Having been abandoned as a child, separated from his older sister, and passed from foster home to foster home for several years before being adopted, it was hard for him to grasp a lasting love and grace-filled love, being accepted for who he was. Though outwardly he was the life of the party, reaching out to others, always cheering for the underdog and known as a peacemaker and a fair person, inwardly he fought rejection, failure, and depression, sabotaging his own success.

After receiving the true knowledge and revelation of grace, knowing he was loved by God, he was so driven to share it with others. When I was battling this disease, he became an example of Jesus. As my situation worsened, I learned to receive more and more. When I would comment on his doing so much and being so joyful and excited about doing so, he said he was grateful to be able to give back after taking so many years. That he was replacing the old, condemning thoughts Satan had used against him with new, positive thoughts and memories to replace them.

He researched ways to make my coping with the illness easier. I never experienced the self-pity and feeling sorry for myself, and I am confident the love and positive reinforcement I received from family members each and every day contributed greatly toward that.

That day in April when I phoned home to talk with him, my daughter answered the telephone. She asked, "Who told you?"

I said I was just calling to talk with dad.

She said, "He's gone."

I asked where, and during her hesitation, I could hear the sirens in the background. Then she said, "No, I mean, he's gone," and I responded by saying, "You mean he's dead?"

She said, "Yes."

I said, "Are you sure?"

She said, "Yes, mom, I'm sure. I found him…" We continued our conversation for a few minutes, then it took me well over an hour to get home because I was out of town and my sister made arrangements to drive me.

When I arrived home, the coroner's vehicle was in the driveway, and my daughter met me outside to tell me what to expect once I entered the house. There were many police officers quietly observing, assuring the body would not be taken until I arrived. When I entered the house, there was such a presence of peace. I walked to my husband, held his hand, kissed his cheek, and the presence of the glory of the Lord was stronger than I had ever known it. It was as though I had the choice to call him back or let him go. After pressing into Jesus, I said, I can't ask him to come back now; he's seen too much. The reality of the invisible being much greater than the visible was so overwhelmingly evident. There was a tangible part of heaven in my house. I know there were many angels in that place, along with a great cloud of witnesses. Their presence was so real—more real than what was evident to the human eye. I realized later the importance of my choice to release him, to let him go, seeing him in Glory with Jesus. I didn't realize I had demonstrated such a totally selfless act until God revealed it to me later. I had not considered myself—how I would function or what I would do without him. I only saw his personality and his desires. In the empty, lonely times, I chose to go to God with thanksgiving and praise for the knowledge of his eternal life; that my husband was in glory with Jesus cheering us on. Knowing he had finished his race here on earth and that I had been a part of that allowed me to continue in thanksgiving, celebration, and genuine gratitude as I transitioned into a life on earth without him.

The Lord provided physical and emotional strength during the following days. During the funeral service, as I sat and looked at the casket, I saw myself walk up to it and climb inside with my husband. It was not a negative or depressive spirit. After reflecting on it many, many times, I believe the Lord was showing me that I was dead to this world. I would live in His Word, His invisible world, His kingdom on earth as it is in heaven, and the things of this world would be of no affect. He showed me so supernaturally how a span of time passes, and I can continue in His will on earth as it is in heaven.

Jesus rushed right in with peace, comfort, and courage. I was so broken; a part of me was missing and I could not explain it or even grasp it fully myself. Seeking the Lord only is where I found comfort. My mind and physical body were numb, incapable of functioning; but His spirit was alive in me. I had to rely on Him for each step, and I remain so grateful. Perhaps that is exactly what He was showing me when I saw myself climb in the casket—He knew how it would be for me in the natural, and He promises to never leave us or forsake us. When we draw near to Him, He draws near to us. I had a hunger and thirst for the Lord greater than ever.

Truth is all I wanted. God began to show me, correct me, and purify my heart. It was as though because my husband and I were one, rather than my losing him, a window of heaven had opened, and I was sharing the glory he was now a part of. I was reminded of the promises connected to the tithe in Malachi 3:10.

"Bring all the tithes into the storehouse, That there may be food in My house, And try me now in this, Says the Lord of hosts, If I will not open for you the windows of Heaven And pour out for you such blessing That there will not be room enough to receive it."

Seek Him First

I knew to continue to "seek Him first and all these things would be added"—my healing, as well as answers to what I would do with my future here on this earth. I knew it would be serving God; there was no reason to be here otherwise. I had no interest in the things of this world. Of course, I desired to see my kids and grandkids grow and prosper and to be a part of their lives. I certainly was not going to take from their lives and be a distraction to what God had called them to do by requiring them to care for me. So my journey to healing continued.

God was faithful, providing counsel, comfort, peace, joy, and most significantly in that time, courage. The joy of the Lord was my strength. I remember having a genuine smile and the thought, *if you smile, they will think you didn't love Earl* (my husband). Immediately turning to God, I understood that if they truly knew me, they knew I loved Earl. It was over that quickly, and I reflected on a time years earlier in my life. As I was driving to work one morning, I was quickened by the Holy Spirit to look in the rearview mirror at myself. Questionably, I looked at myself in the mirror. My response was, I've lost my smile. Knowing the Lord had gotten my attention, I said, "God, I'm sorry. You gave me a smile and I let the world take it away." After acknowledging it and repenting for it, now I knew I had to put forth the effort to get it back. It was a forced smile at first. I very awkwardly practiced smiling all the way to work. As I approached people, answered the phone, or just sat alone with my job duties, the Holy Spirit would bring it to my remembrance, and I would respond by practicing my smile. I did not smile because I felt like it; it was only out of obedience. I practiced and practiced until it became comfortable once again. Later when I looked up the definition of the word smile in the dictionary, I found the following: "smile away; to get rid of by smiling; as he smiled away his tears."

I knew not to look to man for approval but to stay fixed on God's Word.

I realized the skepticism I carried toward some evangelists was a form of pride. I was to begin looking for His anointing, acknowledge His work, and not look at the person. My opinion did not matter. His Word and His work did.

I remain so grateful for restoration. God restores all things. All I have are good memories of our marriage. It's only when others speak of past hurts, troubles, and/or problems that I remember. Even then, it is as though it was not a reality but a story of sorts. When forgiveness is from the heart in response to true repentance, it truly is forgotten. I did not even realize it; but, as events and situations were brought to my remembrance by others, I knew.

> Therefore, as the elect of God, holy and beloved, put on tender mercies, kindness, humility, meekness, longsuffering; bearing with one another, and forgiving one another, if anyone has a complaint against another; even as Christ forgave you, so you also must do. (Colossians 3:12–13 NKJ)

GOOD WILL TOWARD MEN

The first thing the angels tell us when Jesus was born as a baby on this earth is "Glory to God in the Highest and on earth, peace, goodwill toward men!" (Luke 2:14).

The angels sang praise to God in heaven and followed Jesus to earth to praise Him. ("If you've seen Me, you've seen My Father." John 14:9b).

Although He left His glory in heaven and came to earth as a baby, the angels were fixed on praising Him. Glory to God in heaven and glory to God on earth! In Joshua 2:11, Rahab acknowledged Joshua's God as "the Lord your God, He is God in Heaven above and on earth beneath."

He left His home in heaven to tell us and to demonstrate to us His Father's peace and goodwill toward men. Jesus was the peace offering—the One to tell us the will of God for men is good. "For God so loved the world that He gave His Only begotten Son, that whoever believes in Him should not perish but have everlasting life" (John 3:16). Jesus said to His disciples, "My food is to do the will of Him who sent Me, and to finish His work"(John 4:34). Now Jesus would become the "once for all blood sacrifice" (Hebrews 9:10). The sacrifice for all men, all sin, all sickness, disease, pain, need—ALL. "He took our infirmities and bore our sicknesses and diseases" (Matthew 8:17).

Ephesians 5:17 tells us not to be unwise but to understand what the will of the Lord is. As the will of God prospered in Jesus's hand, it was in good works.

I pressed into the word of God, determined to take it by force, knowing the kingdom of God is within us. "Greater is He that is in me than he that is in the world." I shut out the world as much as possible and pressed into the Word. I received a hunger and thirst for the Word greater than I'd ever known.

To build myself up in spirit, I reviewed the will of God.

> Do not conform any longer to the pattern of this world, but be transformed by the renewing of

your mind. Then you will be able to test and approve what God's will is—His good, pleasing, and perfect will. (Romans 12:2)

Therefore do not be unwise, but understand what the will of the Lord is. (Colossians 4:5–6)

Be very careful, then, how you live—not as unwise but as wise, making the most out of every opportunity, because the days are evil. Therefore, do not be foolish, but understand what the Lord's will is. Do not get drunk on wine which leads to debauchery. Instead, be filled with the Spirit. Speak to one another with psalms, hymns, and spiritual songs. Sing and make music in your heart to the lord, always giving thanks to God the Father for everything, in the name of our Lord Jesus Christ. Submit to one another out of reverence for Christ. (Ephesians 15–21)

This is the confidence we have in approaching God: that if we ask anything according to His will, he hears us. And if we know that He hears us—whatever we ask— we know that we have what we asked of Him. (1 John 5:14–15)

You are worthy, our Lord and God, to receive glory and honor and power, for you created all things, and by Your will they were created and have their being. (Revelations 4:11)

Teach me to do Your will, for You are my God; may Your good Spirit lead me on level ground. (Psalms 143:10)

Yet it was the Lord's will to crush Him and cause Him to suffer and though the Lord makes His life a guilt offering and prolong His days, and the will of the Lord will prosper in His hand. (Isaiah 53:10)

Your kingdom come, Your will be done on earth as it is in Heaven. (Matthew 6:10) In this, we see equality or sameness.

Going a little farther, He fell with His face to the ground and prayed, My Father, if it is possible, may this cup be taken from me. Yet, not as I will, but as You will. (Matthew 26:39)

In breaking down this verse by looking at some of the key words, I learned that

- the word *if* means *because, on account of, though*;
- the word *possible* also means *permissible*;

- the word *may* originally meant *ability* or *power*; and
- the word *as* is a weakened form of *also, quite so, just as.*

Then I wrote the verse as follows: My Father, though it is permissible for this cup to be taken from me, I have the ability, the power, to have this cup taken from me, yet Your will is my first desire (demonstrating sameness of spirit).

In summarizing the above scriptures, I said the following: "Glory to God in the Highest and on earth; peace, good will to men. Your will be done on earth as it is in heaven. His will is good, pleasing, and perfect. Be filled with the Spirit. Always give thanks to God in everything, in the name of our Lord Jesus Christ." If we ask anything according to His will, we know He hears us—whatever we ask—and we know we have what we ask of Him. By His will we were created, as were all things, and He is worthy to receive glory, and honor, and power. Teach me to do Your will, for You are my God. May Your good spirit lead me on level ground.

Immediately, I saw balance when reading the words, level ground. Not extreme one direction or the other, but stable, grounded, and sure. Confident my God is who He says He is and unshakable concerning the truth in His Word.

MADE WORTHY

We are made worthy by receiving Jesus. Confessing that He is the Son of God and repenting, his death, burial, and resurrection makes us worthy to receive. "A laborer is worthy of his wages. Forget not any of His benefits." Of course, "the sting of death is gone." We know "to be absent from the body is to be present with Christ." We have no fear of death, but we are worthy through Jesus to be healed, to have our needs met, to walk in health and prosperity, to enjoy walking in the fruit of the Spirit, to have a long life, wholeness. It's all about what God made available to us through His Son, Jesus! It has nothing to do with who we are, what we are, or what we have or have not accomplished. It only matters what we believe and act on and whether we turn to God in our time of need. We don't have to accept what the world puts on us. We endure it for a time. "Many are the afflictions of the righteous, but the Lord delivers them out of them all. Satan comes to steal, kill, and destroy but Jesus came to give life and life more abundantly."

Facts are facts, and truth is truth. I remember seeking after proper words concerning the condition of fibromyalgia. So very clearly one day, I knew to simply say I had been diagnosed with fibromyalgia when I was approached by others concerning my appearance. Never did I speak of the condition unless approached with questions and concerns from others. Being diagnosed with the disease was a fact. Truth, however, is truth; and I knew I was healed and would be whole once again.

STATE OF FORGIVENESS

*If we confess our sins he is faithful and just to forgive
us our sin and to cleanse us from all unrighteousness.*
—1 John 1:9

After repentance, knowing the will of God, knowing we are made worthy not by works but by grace, it is a gift. We must choose to forgive. Just as I chose to smile, I chose to forgive. I did not have to feel like it. I did not even have to want to do it. It was a simple act of obedience. Psalms 66:10b says, "You have refined us as silver is refined." Just as silver is refined, God caused me to cross paths with an individual I had not seen in years, and the impurity came to the surface. I realized I harbored hard feelings, and I found it necessary to repent. I confessed to God—only God—the choice to forgive based on obedience to follow His word. I knew to walk in forgiveness, not taking offense, even if and when the act was committed maliciously or seemingly destructive. God knows the truth and He vindicates. Vengeance is His. He is faithful. He is just. Afterward, when confronted with the thought of that person or offense, I chose to reflect on the time when I made the choice to act in obedience, to acknowledge the unforgiveness, to repent, and to forgive. There is no condemnation in Jesus Christ. Satan is the accuser; Satan destroys. I choose to remember the time and place when I chose to forgive; I will not take it back and give in to the temptation of thinking or dwelling on the offense. I made the choice to walk in forgiveness. Just as I reflect on the time of my salvation to know I am a child of God, I reflect on the time I chose to forgive to walk in freedom and liberty from guilt and condemnation. Resist the devil and he will flee. A portion of the Lord's Prayer in Matthew 6:12 says, "And forgive us our debts, as we forgive our debtors." Then in verse fourteen, "For if you forgive men their trespasses, your heavenly Father will also forgive you." What a great promise in return for a simple act of obedience. Most importantly, it brings us such confidence when we approach God concerning any circumstance or situation.

Then I reflected on another time in my life—a time when I was so wronged. I was very earnestly praying regarding the situation; I was deeply hurt and sorrowful. I wanted people to know the truth, asking God to work in the other person's life. I could have allowed it to escalate and cause great relationship problems. I wanted God to work in the other person's life or expose the other individual. Then, a much unexpected occurrence—God placed in my heart His forgiveness, love, and care for that person. Afterward, I was released from every care of what anyone else might think. The situation did not affect me. I could walk in love and confidence without being concerned about the other person's actions or what anyone else thought or believed to be true.

FAITH-ACTION

If you are willing and obedient, you
shall eat the good of the land.

—Isaiah 1:19

As I slept one night, I saw in a dream the Bible which was opened to the book of Hebrews 11. I could see every word and followed along as I listened to the words being read. When I awoke, I had a hunger to review the act of faith demonstrated by each of those individuals.

There is one common thread I continued to see—obedience and walking with God:

- Enoch pleased God and walked with God (Genesis 6:21–24). Hebrews 11:6 says, "Those who diligently seek Him believe that He Is and that He Is a Rewarder."

- Noah forsook the world and obeyed God (Genesis 6:8–22). Genesis 6:22 reads, "Thus Noah did; according to all that God commanded him so he did." Genesis 7:5 reads "And Noah did according to all that the Lord commanded him." He put his faith into action and became heir of righteousness. God saved Noah's household.

- Abraham obeyed. He was steadfast. When God spoke to Isaac in Genesis 26:4–5, He said, "In your seed all the nations of the world shall be blessed; because, Abraham obeyed My voice and kept My charge, My commandments, My statutes, and My laws."

- Jacob was a peaceful (quiet, mild, plain, even-tempered) man (Genesis 25:27). He obeyed his father, Abraham. He was a man of his word. Even when treated wrongfully, he did what he said he would do.

- Gideon built his faith and confidence in the Lord one action step at a time until the point where he could act immediately without question knowing he walked in victory.

At first, Gideon expressed his feelings of unworthiness, lowliness, and inferiority. When the Angel of the Lord appeared to him in Judges 6:12 and said, "The Lord is with you, you mighty man of valor!" Gideon immediately expressed doubt and a sense of being forsaken by the Lord. In Judges 6:6, "the children of Israel had cried out to the Lord and the Lord appeared to Gideon."

> Then the children of Israel did evil [we see in Judges 6:10 the evil referred to is disobedience] in the sight of the Lord. So the Lord delivered them into the hand of Midian for seven years, and the hand of Midian prevailed against Israel. Because of the Midianites, the children of Israel made for themselves the dens, the caves, and the strongholds which are in the mountains. So it was, whenever Israel had sown, Midianites would come up; also, Amalekites and the people of the East would come up against them. Then,

they would encamp against them and destroy the produce of the earth as far as Gaza, and leave no sustenance for Israel, neither sheep nor ox nor donkey. For they would come up with their livestock and their tents, coming in as numerous as locusts; both they and their camels were without number; and they would enter the land to destroy it. So Israel was greatly impoverished because of the Midianites, and the children of Israel cried out to the Lord. And it came to pass, when the children of Israel cried out to the Lord because of the Midianites, that the Lord sent a prophet to the children of Israel, who said to them, "Thus says the Lord God of Israel: I brought you up from Egypt and brought you out of the house of bondage; and I delivered you out of the hand of the Egyptians and out of the hand of all who oppressed you, and drove them out before you and gave you their land. Also I said to you, I Am the Lord your God; do not fear the gods of the Amorites, in whose land you dwell. But you have not obeyed My voice. Now the Angel of the Lord came and sat under the terebinth tree which was in Ophrah, which belonged to Joash the Abiezrite, while his son Gideon threshed wheat in the winepress, in order to hide it from the Midianites. (Judges 6:1–11)

Gideon was threshing wheat in the winepress to hide it (the wheat). He was guarding and protecting the food, which was being devoured by the enemy. He was caring for his people. A valiant character was demonstrated by Gideon. We do not know where he got the wheat to thresh. "The Midianites entered the land to destroy it and left Israel greatly impoverished," yet, Gideon was threshing wheat. Perhaps it was gathered prior to the Midianites' attack; perhaps the remnants were gathered afterward. We only know Gideon was working (doing what he could) to provide for his people. "God knows us better than we know ourselves."

I've heard it said that Gideon was hiding in fear for his life. I see him courageously guarding and protecting the food, processing it in an extremely unlikely location. Gideon did not act in fear even when feeling fearful; rather, he acted with bravery and did what he could. Gideon said to Him,

> O my Lord, if the Lord is with us, why then has all this happened to us? And where are all His miracles which our fathers told us about, saying, 'Did not the Lord bring us up from Egypt?' But now the Lord has forsaken us and delivered us into the hands of the Midianites." Then the Lord turned to him and said, "Go in this might of yours, and you shall save Israel from the hand of the Midianites. Have I not sent you?" So he said to Him, "O my Lord,

how can I save Israel? Indeed my clan is the weakest in Manasseh, and I am the least in my father's house." And the Lord said to him, "Surely I will be with you, and you shall defeat the Midianites as one man. (Judges 6:13–32)

When we walk in His Word, we have victory!

God did not acknowledge the questions or the sense of forsakenness.

As we continue to read about Gideon, we see obedience and victory. The questions cease and the words of victory come from a ready tongue.

We must be restored to God. Relationship brings confidence and a boldness to ask; knowing He wants us to be and have all that His Word says we are—all He wants us to be and to have.

God is so gracious! When we do our part, whatever it is in our given situation or circumstance, He is faithful to meet us and make up the difference.

God showed Gideon what the enemy was thinking.

I can so parallel faith of today with that of Gideon. As we obey (work our faith) one action step at a time, we build our confidence and trust. Our relationship grows; questions disappear. We know His Word; therefore, we know we hear His voice.

Obedience pleases God.

We can walk with God today.

Building our relationship with God by walking in simple steps of obedience to His word while maintaining communication with Him brings confidence and trust for each next step in our life. Seek Him first and His righteousness and all these things shall be added.

Job so very clearly comes to the forefront of my mind. He was known as the most upright man of God. When Satan came to steal, kill, and destroy all Job possessed, even his most precious sons and daughters, Job remained loyal. He knew God was God, with all power and authority.

Job 1 tells us that Job was blameless and upright, one who feared God and shunned evil. He had seven sons and three daughters, and his possessions were great so that he was the greatest of all the people of the East.

Job experienced grief, pain, broken-heartedness, hopelessness, helplessness. He experienced depression and self-pity, yet he remained loyal. He knew his God and God showed Himself strong.

In all of this, I noticed Satan's approach. He comes to steal, kill, and destroy. He brings question, doubt, confusion. He strikes and leaves Job to deal with it. Job's resolve in his God's character brought deliverance and God's acknowledgement of Job's integrity (seen in Job 2:3) brought not only deliverance but restoration, doubling everything that Job had before.

CAST CARES

Casting all your care upon Him, for He cares for you.
—1 Peter 5:7 (NKJ)

After my husband's passing from this earth to glory, I was left with a battle concerning mice in our house. He had been diligently setting traps and overseeing the situation. Now I was living alone. Because of the illness, I could not physically get up and down to tend to the traps, nor did I have the strength in my hands to open and set the traps. My muscle strength was so exhausted that it was as though there were no thigh muscles in place. If I bent my knees to get down for any reason, I could not get back up. I attempted stepping up on a chair one day to hang something, and had no response from my thigh muscles. I had to stop playing on the floor with my granddaughter. When our second granddaughter was born, for me to hold her, pillows would be propped around me, and I would lay my hand on her and talk to her. She never knew my pain or awkwardness. I was determined to form a relationship with her so that when I was healed and physically able to interact, she would know me. The Lord in His goodness showed me the importance of laying the groundwork of a relationship. After being healed, I would be able to interact and build on an established relationship and she would never know my inabilities and weaknesses. Again, because of His insight and wisdom, my healing was once again confirmed. He was so gracious; I knew I was healed.

As I was praying one evening, I heard a mouse in the wall, and I began to pray for God's help. I acknowledged that the mice were a source of destruction and God's Word says "no destruction will come near me." As the prayer continued, I expressed my concern regarding a bad odor in my house due to dead mice and my inability to retrieve them from hard-to-reach locations. Then I understood what to do. I would set out the poison, and God would allow the mice to die in easy-to-reach locations. That is what I did! The next day, I purchased the poison, set it in several locations throughout the house, then

I went out of town for a couple nights. The evening of the third day, I returned home. When I opened the door, there in the entryway laid a dead mouse. I experienced a sense of awe, a stillness, and reverent presence. I said, "God, what have you done?" I walked a little farther until I could look to my right into the living room. There I could see mice scattered on the floor. As I was viewing the scene, I heard the word *babies* as a thought. I responded, "Yes, if there are babies show me where they are, or I'll have the same problem again." Immediately I understood to turn and walk down into the family room to the furthermost cushion on the sofa. I removed the cushion and there it was—a nest of five baby mice.

The next day, there were a few more mice. On the third day, my granddaughter discovered a mouse, and I told her the story of how God was helping me get rid of the mice. Upon locating the last mouse, I heard my granddaughter from the other room saying, "Grandma, God left one in here!" All were in easy-to-reach locations. With the help of long-handled grill tongs, I was able to discard each one.

God cares! He is our source for all things. We always have a part and we always must ask Him to do His part based on His word (otherwise, how would we know it came from Him?). We always receive His graciousness and care. He sees our innermost part—He knows our motive, and He is true to His word.

He is our source in every situation. He wants us to place the responsibility on Him. He knows our every care, both great and small. He knows us better than we know ourselves. We don't have to be burdened by the overall situation. He wants to be our source in all things.

STEADFAST AND SURE—
NEVER QUIT

When you've done all to stand, therefore, stand.

Just as Caleb and Joshua never let go of their confidence in God after seeing the Promised Land, we must stay confident in our promises, regardless of the circumstances. Caleb and Joshua saw the promise and never let go. They never allowed the negativity, the pain, or heartache attach to them. They didn't get bitter concerning others' actions.

When it was time for Joshua to lead the way "into the land which God had given to the children of Israel," he was told numerous times to be strong and of good courage. In Joshua 1:9, God speaks to Joshua and says, "Have I not commanded you? Be strong and of good courage; do not be afraid, nor be dismayed, for the Lord your God is with you wherever you go."

> Only be strong and very courageous, that you may observe to do according to all the law which Moses My servant commanded you: do not turn from it to the right hand or to the left, that you may prosper wherever you go. This Book of the Law shall not depart from your mouth, but you shall meditate in it day and night, that you may observe to do according to all that is written in it. For then you will make your way prosperous, and then you will have good success. Have I not commanded you? Be strong and of good courage; do not be afraid, nor be dismayed, for the Lord your God is with you wherever you go. (Joshua 1:7–9)

Whoever rebels against your command and does not heed your words, in all that you command him, shall be put to death. Only be strong and of good courage. Joshua 1:18

Rahab acknowledged Joshua's God as the Lord your God, He is God in heaven above and on earth beneath. Joshua 2:11

Joshua 14:7–11 tells us that Caleb was forty years of age when he went in to spy out the land. He was now eighty-five years of age. He went to Joshua and reminded him, reflected on, that day they went in to spy out the land. Caleb wholly followed the Lord his God in his heart. He remained steadfast and sure for forty-five years. Caleb said in verse 11, "I am as strong this day as on the day that Moses sent me; just as my strength was then, so now is my strength for war, both for going out and for coming in."

He reflected on what Moses said that day when Caleb returned from spying out the land of the giants. So Moses swore on that day, saying, "Surely the land where your foot has trodden shall be your inheritance and your children's forever, because you have wholly followed the Lord my God" (Joshua 14:9).

Caleb acknowledges God for keeping him alive.

In Joshua 14:10, he says, "And now, behold, the Lord has kept me alive, as he said, these 45 years, ever since the Lord spoke this word to Moses while Israel wandered in the wilderness; and now here I am this day, 85 years old."

Hebron became the inheritance of Caleb because he wholly followed the Lord God of Israel. He believed, obeyed, and acted on the word of God.

DELIVERANCE

I come to give life and life more abundantly.

Nahum 1:7–9 reads, "The Lord is good. A stronghold in the day of trouble. And He knows those who trust in Him. But with an overflowing flood He will make an utter end of its place, and darkness will pursue His enemies. What do you conspire against the Lord? He will make an utter end of it. Affliction will not rise up a second time."

Second Timothy 2:19 (Paul to Timothy) reads, "Nevertheless, the solid foundation of God stands, having this seal: 'The Lord knows those who are His,' and, 'Let everyone who names the name of Christ depart from iniquity.'"

> Many are the afflictions of the righteous but the Lord delivers

them out of them all. (Psalms 34:19)

Jesus is the Once for All blood sacrifice. (Hebrews 9:12–10:10)

They overcame him by the blood of the Lamb and by the word of their testimony. (Revelation 12:11a)

When he took those stripes on his back, when he was bruised, wounded, punished, he did it for each one of us. "He Himself took our infirmities and bore our sicknesses and diseases" (Matthew 8:17). All suffering, pain, sorrow, grief, broken-heartedness, need, lack, forsakenness, loneliness, depression, and all the negative things of this world were nailed to that cross with Jesus. Jesus was buried in a tomb and was raised again three days later. What was it about His Resurrection? Not only do we have a risen, alive King who loves us, His creation; but we know he defeated ALL on our behalf. Not all the world puts on us can last. We endure for a time.

The name of Jesus is above every name, fibromyalgia included, sorrow included, broken-heartedness included, lack and need included. Jesus came out of that tomb only three days later and there were no signs of his being beaten or punished, no scarring except those nail prints in his hands and feet and the scar in his side where he had been pierced with the sword. Anyone who has ever suffered with a bruise can testify that the signs last for days. Whether it is in discoloration or pain, it is there. When Jesus arose with a glorified body, there were no signs of bruising though he had been beaten beyond recognition. There were no signs of the stripes on his back. There were no signs of the thorns on his head. It was all defeated! Just as every bruise, every cut of the whip, every abused area of his body from head to toe was defeated and wiped away so that there was no sign of it, so was every sin, every sickness and disease, all pain, grief, sorrow, need, all of it. It was gone! All of it for all people. It remains defeated! We acknowledge it—acknowledge Him as the Son of God, our Savior; we make Him our Lord and all His kingdom is ours on earth as it is in heaven. The things of this world are of no affect. When the unseen is greater in us than what is seen, it cannot be taken from us.

God gives life, breath, and all things!

VICTORY—WORTH THE FIGHT!

Feed on the word of God knowing that spiritual revelation is greater and has a much greater reward than we can think or imagine.

I knew without faith it would be impossible to please Him, for he who comes to God must believe that He is a rewarder of those who diligently seek Him. It matters not how we feel, what negative reports are given; we will reap if we do not faint and if we do not grow weary in well-doing.

While watching a praise and worship program on television one evening fourteen months after the diagnosis of fibromyalgia, the pain disappeared. I had my hands lifted in the air in praise; I did not feel anything—just the absence of pain. The following morning when I woke up and began moving, my every joint began popping. From head to toe, I made every effort to use various joints. Each time, there was popping. I believe the inflammation encircling the joints had been relieved, allowing them to move back into proper position. I continued in praise and thanksgiving, sharing only with my closest family members who had been so faithful and loving during my battle.

While the pain was gone and my mobility had greatly improved due to my joint structure, I remained extremely weak and experienced great muscle fatigue. My muscles were so nearly exhausted I could hardly tell they existed. I continued with warm water therapy sessions. When it was time to get out of the water, I called on all that was within me for the ability and grace to exit the pool. Fortunately, a ramp was built into the pool. I remember how heavy my body was. Inch by inch, I would make my way out of the pool. It would have been so much simpler to take that wheelchair ride up the ramp and to the shower. I knew if I could stay focused, continue to smile, concentrate on my mind's eye rather than how I felt, I would make it. Determination and grace took me from the pool to the shower.

The day after the praise and worship program, I noticed on the calendar of events scrolling on the television screen that a healing evangelist was scheduled to be in the local area. When the Holy Spirit quickened me to attend, my response was, "Really?" After spending time with God, I soon understood that my attitude of skepticism toward some evangelists had escalated to a prideful level. Though I know to be watchful that words and actions line up with the Word of God, I had allowed pride to judge before listening. If it seemed theatrical or emotional, I turned my back to it. I am to look at the anointing (God's work being demonstrated) and, most importantly, be accountable for my own attitude and actions. I was reminded of Jesus saying to Peter, "What is that to you?" In John 21:21–22, Peter said to Jesus, "But Lord, what about this man?" Jesus said, "Peter, what is that to you? You follow Me."

I thanked God for His continued work in me concerning a pure heart (bringing those impurities to the surface so I could deal with them). After repenting for my attitude, I was obedient in arranging to attend. During the praise and worship session of the event, I partook wholeheartedly. It was as though no one else was present. And it happened! During the praise and worship, I was made whole.

I hesitate to describe it because the last thing I want to do is encourage someone to look for a feeling rather than to seek God first. God knows us better than we know ourselves. He knows how to best work His Plan in us. I share this because I want to glorify Him and His work in me. Although if I had been seeking after a certain person or a particular feeling, I am convinced I would have missed my healing altogether. It is in relationship with God, in diligently seeking Him, that we are made whole. Simple and sure is His Way.

As I stood with my hands and arms lifted, praising God, there began a simultaneous action of wind and oil. It was as an electrical wind current beginning in the very center of my bones and pushing outward against the inside of my skin. At the same time, a thickened warm substance like oil or honey was being poured downward on the inside of me. I had no outward feeling. Slowly, consistently together, beginning at my fingertips and continuing to the floor, I experienced the flow of wind and oil.

I see it as the threshing of the wheat when the waste, the chaff, was blown away and the healing balm as it soothed and made whole.

I had been so totally absorbed in praise and worship; I had not heard anything. Just after that experience, I heard the evangelist say, "Don't wait for me to call it out. If the Lord has touched you, get down here." I immediately turned to my daughter and said I need to go down there. When we reached the gate at the foot of the stairs, we were told we needed to go back to the top of the seating section, cross over, and go back down the other side. We turned and I climbed very rapidly to the top of the seating section. Part of the way up, I remember my daughter taking my hand. As we turned to walk across behind the seating section, I turned to my daughter and told her I had felt as light as a feather coming up those stairs. She said she thought I was going to take off and leave her, which was a very understandable response. Beforehand, I had to take one stair step at a time—one foot and then the other foot onto the same step, requiring support and a push or support upward. My family always did this in such a subtle, inconspicuous manner demonstrating respect and allowing me to maintain my dignity. I will always be grateful for the manner in which they treated me. They were continually aware and helpful as needed but never acknowledging my weaknesses or the disease in any way. I saw myself healed, and they honored that in their speech and their actions.

When we stepped onto the floor, we discussed my story briefly with a gentleman who met us there. I was asked if I could do anything now that I could not do before. I stood quietly for a moment. Not thinking about the stairs, I bent over and touched the floor. My daughter responded by saying, "She couldn't do that before!"

Jesus has truly been like a brother and a best friend, and the Holy Spirit has been faithfully with me. The revelation of Jesus being closer than a brother is so very real to me. I am fortunate to have five brothers and any one of them would do anything in their power and ability to help me in any way possible. I have no question, no doubt concerning that; therefore, Jesus being closer than a brother and our Father, God, having all power over all things, gives me total victory over every situation.

A few days following my healing, I had a doctor's appointment. I shared my healing experience with him. He remarked that he had noticed my mobility and rapid pace when I entered the office. He was impressed and wondered what the situation was. We talked for a while, and after the examination, he officially discontinued all medications. As we walked out of the office into the hallway, he commented that God is the greatest physician of all, and I thanked him for treating me with such respect and dignity during the process. That could be considered my exit interview.

One week later, I visited the physical therapist. After I shared my experience with her, she retested my pain levels and range of motion. I had increased from near-zero percentage of movement to full range of motion and had no pain.

The Lord is my justice. Psalms 37:6 says, "He shall bring forth your righteousness as the light, and your justice as the noonday." Then, in Romans 12:19, "Beloved do not avenge yourselves, but rather give place to wrath; for it is written, Vengeance is Mine, I will repay, says the Lord."

About the Author

Debbie was married for twenty-eight years to her late husband, Earl. She and Earl had two daughters. She now has five grandchildren and two great granddaughters. She experienced much transition after her husband's passing. First, pursuing and receiving her healing; then, working as an office manager, executive assistant, and earning her certified administrative professional certificate. Finally, she earned her Oklahoma realtor license.

CPSIA information can be obtained
at www.ICGtesting.com
Printed in the USA
FSHW012325230421
80652FS

9 781648 019722